The Prophetic Almanac 2024

By

Pastor Bill Jenkins

The Prophetic Almanac 2024

By Pastor Bill Jenkins

Manufactured in the
United States of America
ISBN # 979-8-218-32455-1

Published by
B&B Media
Upland, California
Visit the author's website at:
www.pastorbilljenkins.org

TABLE OF CONTENTS

Introduction

I am proud to say I have been releasing information, inspiration, and divine revelation through the *Prophetic Almanac* series for a full decade which makes this 2024 *Prophetic Almanac* the 10th anniversary edition. The goal has always been to give the people of God a spiritual alternative to the secular *Farmer's Almanac* and to release a vision for that specific God-given vision every year. A vision is a spiritual picture for the future that guides our actions. A vision produces a clear path towards our destination. A vision is a revelation from God that gives direction, provides clarity and produces hope. The Bible says in Proverbs 29:18 that *"without a vision, people will perish."* Perishing is not just dying physically; it is dying spiritually. We die and live unfulfilled lives when we have no vision. Having a vision from God is important because…

- It gives us a strategic plan for success.
- It gives us direction, so we know where we are headed.
- It gives us something to invest our time in rather than wasting our time.

- It gives us the ability to believe in something bigger than ourselves.
- It gives us the opportunity to stay focused instead of being sidetracked and double-minded.
- It gives us a sense of purpose.

God made each of us with both physical and spiritual eyes. Although our physical eyes are amazing in so many ways, they have significant limitations. They can only see physical reality and are useless when it comes to perceiving a spiritual reality. So, this book will take you on a journey to help you discover the vision for 2024 and open your eyes to the supernatural. It is not an understatement to say 2024 is a critical year. It is an election year. It is an Olympic year. It is a leap year. On April 8, 2024, we will experience a total solar eclipse when the moon passes between the sun and earth, completely blocking the face of the sun. It is a year that will bring surprises and changes. It is a year where there will be surprise changes. This will be a year like no other. Although the secular media will not give an honest assessment of the economy, the recession will continue for at least the first half of the year. Interest in artificial intelligence (AI) will continue to increase but look for a major glitch in its development that will produce a worldwide scare in 2024. Wars and rumors of wars will continue to plague our society. Earthquakes, fires, floods, hurricanes, tornadoes, and other natural disasters will dominate the headlines. The unknowns and underdogs will be the story of the Olympics. Politically, expect the unexpected, and know the next four years will be nothing like the last four years. There will be more "breaking news" than ever before in 2024. Spiritually, it is simple. God wants us to keep our eyes on Him as the distractions and deceptions of this world continue to increase. As always, I will give you everything from A to Z that is relevant to the number 24 in order to release a vision that reflects the heart of God for this year. Some things I share may create anxiety or apprehension, but do not let it cause fear. God is in control and gives us strength, not weakness. God reveals to help and heal, so the revelation of this book is designed to help you have the best year of your life as you walk in obedience to God. God's plan and vision is to bless the faithful in 2024.

"For I know the thoughts that I think toward you, saith the Lord, thoughts of peace, and not of evil, to give you an expected end." Jeremiah 29:11

Chapter 1
Preview

Previews are much like movie trailers. They do not give you all the details of what is to come, but they give you enough of an overview of what is to come. In this chapter, I give you just some things and people to be looking out for in 2024. All these things are designed to help you become more spiritually sensitive. Look for these things in the news and other media and connect them to the vision of 2024.

Sport of the Year
Summer Olympics

State of the Year
On August 10, 1821, Missouri became the 24th State of the Union

City of the Year
St. Louis, Missouri
It is the 24th largest city by population in the United States of America as of 2023 according to macrotrends.net

Planet of the Year
Mars

Bible Characters of the Year
Men - Luke
Women - Phoebe
Youth - Daniel

Bible Story of the Year
Woman with the Alabaster Box
Luke 7:36-50

Scripture of the Year
"And when he had taken the book, the four beasts and four and twenty elders fell down before the Lamb, having every one of them harps, and golden vials full of odours, which are the prayers of saints." Revelation 5:8

Book of the Bible of the Year
Luke

Fruit of the Spirit of the Year
Love

Gift of the Spirit of the Year
Discernment

Word of the Year
Worship

Color of the Year
Light blue

Super Food of the Year
Blueberries

Vegetable of the Year
Carrots

Snack of the Year
Apples

Geographical Places of the Year
- France   - New Zealand
- USA   - Iran
- Israel   - Norway
- South Africa   - China
- India

Animal of the Year
Bear

General Characteristics of a Bear

<u>Positive</u>	<u>Negative</u>
– Thick skin	– Unpredictable
– Strong	– Territorial
– Great memories	– Promiscuous
– Family-oriented	– Cruel
– Courageous	– Insensitive
– Confident	– Quick-tempered
– Protective	– Emotional
	– Not always friendly

Bears are definitely animals that are mentioned several times in the Bible. David protected the sheep from bears when they were attacked in the fields. Isaiah said we growl like bears when we are in mourning. Two female bears killed 42 children when they mocked the prophet in 2 Kings. Daniel prophesied of a nation with the symbol of a bear rising up to create problems in the end-times. Russia is associated with a bear.

What Kind of Bear Will You Choose
to Be in 2024?

Grizzly Bear = They are the biggest and strongest of all bears. Fast runners, light sleepers, and unfriendly in their personalities.

Koala Bear = They are loving, caring, and family-oriented animals who love to eat.

Polar Bear = They are determined to get what they want and refuse to be denied. They do not need to be entertained or taken care of in any way. They are great hunters.

Panda Bear = They are very cute, cuddly, and adorable animals. However, they are not the most communicative bears, and their personalities are not the best. They do not play well with others.

Teddy Bear = They are warm, loyal, friendly, never bite, or say a bad word. They listen to all your cares and are totally dependable.

24 People to Watch in 2024

1. Benjamin Netanyahu, Israel Prime Minister
2. Kiefer Sutherland, Actor
3. Bruno Mars, Singer
4. Tom Selleck, Actor
5. Patrick Mahomes, NFL Quarterback
6. Harrison Ford, Actor
7. Donald Trump, President
8. Ice Cube, Rapper
9. Elon Musk, Entrepreneur
10. Kevin Hart, Comedian
11. Clarence Thomas, Supreme Court Justice
12. Victor Wembanyama, NBA Rookie
13. Katie Ledecky, Olympic Gold Medalist
14. Tim Scott, U.S. Senator
15. Gavin Newsom, Politician
16. Ryan Reynolds, Actor
17. Ken Griffey Jr, MLB Hall of Famer
18. Joe Biden, President
19. Giannis Antetokounmpo, NBA Player
20. Tim Cook, Apple CEO
21. Nikki Haley, Politician
22. Joaquin Phoenix, Actor
23. Connor Bedard, NHL Player
24. Ron DeSantis, Florida Governor

Prophetic Dates of the Year

1. Wednesday, January 24, 2024
2. Saturday, February 24, 2024
3. Sunday, March 24, 2024
4. Wednesday, April 24, 2024
5. Friday, May 24, 2024
6. Monday, June 24, 2024
7. Wednesday, July 24, 2024
8. Saturday, August 24, 2024
9. Tuesday, September 24, 2024
10. Thursday, October 24, 2024
11. Sunday, November 24, 2024
12. Tuesday, December 24, 2024

24 Movies of the Year

With the actors' strike concluding at the end of 2023, these movies could be moved or rescheduled at any time.

1. Deadpool 3
2. Gladiator 2
3. Joker: Folie à Deux
4. Snow White
5. Winnie-the-Pooh: Blood and Honey 2
6. Wicked
7. Captain America: Brave New World

8. The Fall Guy
9. Kingdom of the Planet of the Apes
10. Bad Boys 4
11. Kung Fu Panda 4
12. Thunderbolts
13. The Lord of the Rings: The War of the Rohirrim
14. Madame Web
15. Bob Marley: One Love
16. The Electric State
17. The Passion of the Christ: Resurrection
18. Mufasa: The Lion King
19. Transformers One
20. Mission: Impossible – Dead Reckoning Part 2
21. Wise Guys
22. Ordinary Angels
23. Garfield
24. Imaginary Friends

Chapter 2
Fun Facts

General

- The Roman Numeral is XXIV.
- At 24 weeks, a baby in the womb is about the size of an ear of corn.
- An icositetragon is a regular polygon with 24 sides.
- Four and Twenty was an American racehorse.
- The atomic number chromium is 24.
- 24 degrees Celsius is 75.2 Fahrenheit.
- 24 degrees Fahrenheit is -4.444 degrees Celsius.
- The number 24 represents the number of hours in a day.
- The number 24 represents the number of karats in 100% pure gold.
- The number 24 is the number of letters in the Greek alphabet.
- The number 24 represents the number of frames per second at which a motion picture film is projected.
- The number 24 is the number of points on a backgammon board.
- 24 Hour fitness is a gym open 24 hours.

Sports

- Famous Sports Players to wear #24 Jersey:
  o Ken Griffey Jr., Baseball
  o Kobe Bryant, Basketball
  o Willie Mays, Baseball
  o Rickey Henderson, Baseball
  o Barry Bonds, Baseball
  o Bill Bradley, Basketball
  o Charles Woodson, Football
  o Chris Chelios, Hockey
- Jeff Gordan drove the #24 car in Nascar.
- The NBA has a 24 second shot clock.
- In 2015 and 2019, the FIFA Soccer World Cup had 24 national teams featured in the finals.

Entertainment

- "Twenty-four" was a song by the band Switchfoot that expresses deep despair and dismay at having reached twenty-four and found that life is not what you thought it would be.
- *24* was a television drama that ran for 9 seasons.
- James Dean, Lee Harvey Oswald, and Chandra Levy all died at the early age of 24.
- "24K Magic" is a song released by Bruno Mars in 2016.

- A24 is an independent entertainment company that specializes in film and television.

History

- In 1964, the 24th Amendment prohibited states from requiring a poll tax as a condition for voting in federal elections.
- Stephen Grover Cleveland (March 18, 1837-June 24, 1908) was an American politician who served as the 22nd and 24th president of the United States from 1885 to 1889 and 1893 to 1897.

Biblical

- In Revelation 4:4, 24 elders sat on 24 thrones.
- The word "worship" is mentioned nine times, and the word "worshipped" is mentioned 15 times totaling 24 times in the book of Revelation.
- Jotham and Boaz are both mentioned in the Bible 24 times.
- Joshua, 2 Samuel, and The Gospel of Luke all have 24 chapters.
- In 2 Samuel 21, there was a giant that had 6 fingers on each hand and each foot, giving him a total of 24 fingers/toes on his body.

- Although the book of Luke only has 24 chapters, it has more words than Acts, which has 28 chapters. Therefore, it is correct to say that Luke is the longest New Testament book. Luke has 24 chapters and 1,151 verses. The book of Acts has 28 chapters but only has 1,007 verses. Although Matthew also has 28 chapters, it only has 1,071 verses.
- Baasha, the third ruler of the Kingdom of Israel, reigned for twenty-four official years.
- Around God's heavenly throne are 24 elders, each wearing a crown and sitting on a throne, who will assist Him in governing the universe after the tribulation. (Rev. 4:1 - 4).
- The following words are mentioned 24 times in the Bible:
    - Bridegroom
    - Dedicated
    - Dogs
    - Female
    - Northward
    - Synagogues
    - Tithes
- The word "water" is mentioned 24 times in the Gospel of John.
- The words "believe", "believeth", and "believed" are each used eight times totaling 24 times in the book of Romans.
- Psalm 72 lists 24 things that Jesus Christ, as High Priest after the order of Melchizedek,

will do when He sits upon His throne and rules as King and Priest during the Millennium. They are the following:

1. He will righteously judge the people.
2. He will judge, with justice, the poor and needy.
3. Peace will be brought by the mountains.
4. Small hills shall also experience peace.
5. He shall judge the poor.
6. He shall save the children of the needy.
7. Those who oppress Israel will be crushed.
8. He shall rule like rain upon grass.
9. He shall rule like the water that showers the globe.
10. He will cause the righteous to flourish.
11. He will bring the righteous an abundance of peace.
12. He shall rule from sea to sea.
13. He shall rule from the river unto the ends of the earth.
14. When he hears the needy cry out, he will deliver him.
15. The poor and those who have no help will also be delivered.
16. Those who are needy and weak will receive compassion.
17. The lives of those in need will be saved.
18. The needy, who are oppressed and experience violence, will be redeemed.

19. The blood of those in need will be precious in His sight.
20. He will cause an abundance of grain on the earth.
21. He will bring an abundance of fruit.
22. He will make those of the city flourish like grass.
23. He will make His name to be continued.
24. He will bless all men.

- The number 24 is mentioned 19 times in the Bible.

Chapter 3
2024 Vision

In developing a vision for a specific year, I am trying to find the heart of God or the will of God for that year. A vision guides us and directs us forward into our future. Getting a vision means getting the precise plan of God that will propel us into completing our purpose on earth. Actually putting the vision in action in our lives is what sets us up for success and sets us apart from others. In my searching for direction, I always begin by looking at the scriptures in the Bible that reference the number for that year. Obviously, this year I am looking for the number 24 and when it is mentioned in scripture. I am finding the higher I go up in numbers, the lower probability it is mentioned much in the Word. Twenty-four is mentioned 19 times in the Bible, so now the hunt begins to find the heart of God for 2024. In researching the number 24, at least six of the 19 references to the number 24 mentioned in the Bible reveal the common thread of … worship.

I do not tell God what the vision is, He tells me. He reveals His will by what the scriptures say that contain the number 24. So, the vision for 2024 is worshiping God. Also the words "worship" or "worshipped" are mentioned 24 times in the book of Revelation. Worship is a spiritual word, a scriptural word, and even an end-time word. I am not flying by the seat of my pants or guessing to come up with something. I am making a calculated spiritual conclusion that worshiping God should be our focus in 2024. Worshiping God would definitely be something that is consistently scriptural to follow and obey. So, worship is the vision for 2024. It is only a seven-letter word, but its meaning gives us several avenues to investigate to understand this concept of worship. Make no mistake, whenever I refer to worship, it is always connected to God. Worship is not about a person that impresses you or a place that interests you or even a thing that inspires you. Worship is all about God the Father, the Son, and the Holy Ghost. Worship is defined as showing honor, reverence, and devotion to a divine being or supernatural power. True worship is valuing or treasuring God above all things.

Eight Biblical Facts About Worship

1. God wants us to worship Him.
   "But the hour cometh, and now is, when the true worshippers shall worship the Father in spirit and in truth: for the Father seeketh such to worship him." John 4:23

God desires us to worship Him because He created us specifically to worship Him. Worshiping God proves our longing to be in the presence of God and bring pleasure to the Lord.

2. Worship is the highest form of communication with God.

   "O come, let us worship and bow down: let us kneel before the Lord our maker." Psalm 95:6

   Prayer is great, but most prayers can be selfish. Worship is all about honoring God, not about seeking God for answers. The biggest communication problem is that we often only listen to respond instead of listening to understand. Worship seeks to understand what God is communicating, not to respond to what we do not like.

3. The greatest level of worship is obedience.

   "And Samuel said, Hath the Lord as great delight in burnt offerings and sacrifices, as in obeying the voice of the Lord? Behold, to obey is better than sacrifice, and to hearken than the fat of rams." 1 Samuel 15:22

Obedience is better than sacrifice. Sacrifice is worship, but obedience is the greatest level of worship. It is easy to worship God with a sacrifice. It is not so easy to worship God with our ability to walk in obedience to His commands.

4. Worship is the best way to show our love to God.

"And thou shalt love the Lord thy God with all thy heart, and with all thy soul, and with all thy mind, and with all thy strength: this is the first commandment." Mark 12:30

When you really love someone, you want to do things that make them happy. My wife loves coffee. I love my wife. So, I make coffee for my wife every day because it makes her happy. Worship makes God happy because it proves our love for Him.

5. Worship is spiritual warfare.

"For the weapons of our warfare are not carnal, but mighty through God to the pulling down of strong holds;" 2 Corinthians 10:4

Worship is a weapon that we use in spiritual warfare to defeat the enemy. The walls of Jericho fell because of worship in Joshua 6.

David used worship to remove an evil spirit from Saul in 1 Samuel 16. Paul and Silas opened prison doors by worshiping God in Acts 16. Worship defeats the devil!!!

6. Worshiping God correctly removes lukewarmness.

"Wherefore we receiving a kingdom which cannot be moved, let us have grace, whereby we may serve God acceptably with reverence and godly fear: For our God is a consuming fire." Hebrews 12:28-29

When you worship God correctly it sets a fire in your soul that forces a lukewarm spirit out of your life.

7. Worship gives us a glimpse of Heaven on Earth.

"And the four beasts had each of them six wings about him; and they were full of eyes within: and they rest not day and night, saying, Holy, holy, holy, Lord God Almighty, which was, and is, and is to come. And when those beasts give glory and honour and thanks to him that sat on the throne, who liveth for ever and ever, The four and twenty elders fall down before him that sat on the throne, and worship him that liveth for ever

and ever, and cast their crowns before the throne, saying, Thou art worthy, O Lord, to receive glory and honour and power: for thou hast created all things, and for thy pleasure they are and were created." Revelation 4:8-11

If the angels in Heaven are worshiping, the people on Earth should be worshiping. Humans are higher in authority than angels. We can sing a song of redemption that the angels cannot sing. That is why our worship as humans on Earth should exceed the angels' worship in Heaven.

8. Worshiping God is the #1 fear of the devil.
   "How art thou fallen from heaven, O Lucifer, son of the morning! how art thou cut down to the ground, which didst weaken the nations! For thou hast said in thine heart, I will ascend into heaven, I will exalt my throne above the stars of God: I will sit also upon the mount of the congregation, in the sides of the north: I will ascend above the heights of the clouds; I will be like the most High." Isaiah 14:12-14

Lucifer was the worship leader of Heaven until his pride got in the way because he no longer wanted to give worship to God, he wanted to be like God and receive worship. God replaced Lucifer with humans who would worship Him in spirit and in truth. The devil hates when we worship God because it reminds him of his failure. When we worship God, we do it better than the devil ever could.

Worshiping God is one of the most important and fruitful things we can do as a Christian. It is incumbent upon us to do it correctly. The Bible gives us seven Hebrew words to describe the ways to properly praise and worship the Lord.

Seven Ways to Worship God

Barak = kneel
Halal = brag
Shabach = shout
Tehillah = sing
Towdah = sacrifice
Yadah = raise hands
Zamar = instruments

- Proper worship is kneeling before God.
- Proper worship is bragging about God.
- Proper worship is shouting out to God.
- Proper worship is singing out loud to God.
- Proper worship is putting your flesh in subjection to God.

- Proper worship is raising your hands to God.
- Proper worship is playing instruments for God.

Worship is powerful!!! Worship is a privilege. Worship is a responsibility. Worship is awesome. Worshiping God helps us to complete three important goals:

- Pleasing God
- Improving ourselves
- Overcoming the devil

You are accomplishing a lot more with one act of obedience in worshiping the Lord. So, to keep it simple, remember the who, what, where, when, and why of worship.

> Who of worship?
> > God
> What of worship?
> > Honor
> Where of worship?
> > Anywhere
> When of worship?
> > Now
> Why of worship?
> > Love

There are many other things that the Lord requires of us in 2024. Throughout this book, I will give you scriptures that will help give you direction. I will look at the main messages hidden in the 20 books of the Bible that have a chapter 24 in them. I will reveal other truths that will reveal God's will for your life this year. None of those revelations are more important than worship. Worship is your #1 goal of 2024.

Worship God with your words.
Worship God with your actions.
Worship God with your thoughts.
Worship God with your obedience.

Do not just say you love God; show God you love Him with your total complete devotion through worship. Make worship a priority all 366 days of this year. Honor God and show how much you treasure God by worshiping more in 2024.

Chapter 4
The Bible Speaks

GENESIS 24
FINDING A SPOUSE

This chapter is all about Abraham helping his son find a wife. Abraham was getting old and wanted Isaac to have a good wife before he passed away. Isaac was not as motivated as Abraham wanted him to be, so Abraham began to take matters into his own hands. For a young man, it is important to find the right woman God has for him. A woman can make or break a man's destiny.

"Whoso findeth a wife findeth a good thing, and obtaineth favour of the Lord." Proverbs 18:22

Seven Qualities to Look for in a Godly Wife

1. She cannot be unequally yoked, v.3-4
2. She must be a servant, v.15
3. She has to have spirit of hospitality, v.24-25
4. She has to understand spiritual authority, v.49

5. She must be willing to leave and cleave, v.57-58
6. She has to have respect for her man, v.64-65
7. She must make the man a better person, v.67

It takes more than these characteristics to make a good wife, but this is certainly a great place to start. If you are a young, single man of the proper age to be married, do not be quick to blow off these scriptures. Although this chapter is about a man finding a wife, marriage is just as important to a woman, so these traits work for both parties. Do not go out looking for a partner but allow God to bring someone in your life that you want to be with forever. This could be the year God brings your future spouse into your life.

Find Your Future Spouse In 2024

EXODUS 24
THE FIRE OF GOD

After speaking with Moses through the last several chapters, God tells him to go tell the people of Israel all the commands and laws of the Lord in order to establish a covenant between Israel and God. After Moses told them to make a decision to agree to the terms of God, they all agreed to follow God and obey His commands. Moses built an altar at the foot of Mount Sinai and erected 12 pillars which represented the 12 tribes of Israel. A sacrifice was made, and the blood covenant was basically signed by the people to follow the commands of God. Then Moses returned to the mountain and brought Aaron, Nadab, Abihu, and the 70 elders of the people. They came and worshiped God and ate dinner from a distance. These 74 men saw the "God of Israel", but Moses was called to go up higher on the mountain to get the official Ten Commandments from God as the mediator and to seal the deal with God. As Moses went higher up on the mountain, he saw God's glory which was revealed in a cloud, and Moses dwelt there for six days outside the cloud. On the seventh day, God called him to join Him in the cloud of glory and he remained there 40 days and 40 nights. The Bible says the glory of God on top of the mountain appeared to the people below as a "devouring fire". The fire of God changed Moses in the Old Testament, and the fire of God changed the 120 people in the upper room on the day of Pentecost in the New Testament. The fire of God will change us!!!

I believe God is wanting to release another round of devouring fire to those who are passionately pursuing Him in 2024. God despises lukewarmness and desires us to be on fire for Him. When we seek after more of God, we will not be denied by the Lord. The Bible encourages us to let our fire burn bright in a dark world and to never allow others to quench the fire of the Spirit in our lives. Let this be a year you enter the presence of God, so you can experience the glory of God. In experiencing the glory of God, the fire of God will be released to do three things:

1. Remove all impurities that keep you from drawing closer to God.
2. Create an appetite for God that only the Lord can fill.
3. Allow your flame to burn bright enough for others to be drawn to Jesus.

Do not be half-hearted or lukewarm in your commitment to God. Allow the fire of God to reign in your life.

Pursue the Fire of God More
In 2024

LEVITICUS 24
LOVE WHAT GOD LOVES

Leviticus 24 is a story divided into three parts… the lamp, the loaves, and the loudmouth.

1. The Lamp, v.1-4

    The lamp was in the Holy Place to provide light in the darkness of the tabernacle. According to Leviticus 24, the light must be kept burning at all times and never be allowed to burn out.

2. The Loaves, v.5-9

    Israel had a weekly ceremony called "the changing of the loaves." It took place once a week on the Sabbath. Twelve fresh large loaves were baked on the Sabbath and would replace the old loaves from the previous week. This week-old bread was part of the "holy food" eaten by the priests.

3. The Loudmouth, v.10-23

    The loudmouth was an Egyptian man who got in a fistfight with an Israelite man. We are not told who started the fight or who won the fight, but somewhere in the middle of the fight, the Egyptian man blasphemed God or spoke a curse against the Israelite using the name of God. Blasphemy was a crime punishable by death.

The whole point of this story is to watch your words and never take the name of the Lord in vain. The man who blasphemed was probably running his mouth about the ritualistic ceremony that Israel was doing in the temple. We must be careful not to speak against things we do not fully understand. Blasphemy in many ways is despising what God values. This year do not worry about the loudmouths that speak against things that God values. Focus in on loving what God loves and hating what God hates.

Love What God Loves In 2024

NUMBERS 24
SAY ONLY WHAT GOD WANTS
YOU TO SAY

King Balak offered Balaam the prophet a huge reward in exchange for using his power to curse Israel. Balaam struggled with whether to do it or not. Balak's offer was large, but it would mean saying what King Balak wanted to hear instead of saying what God wanted to be said. Ultimately Balaam decided to go, but he warned King Balak's people saying, "Even if Balak gave me all the silver and gold in his palace, I could not do anything on my own that would go beyond the command of the Lord." He said in verse 13, "I must say only what the Lord says."

"But let your communication be, Yea, yea; Nay, nay: for whatsoever is more than these cometh of evil." Matthew 5:37

We need to speak less and listen more in 2024. When we do speak, let two rules guide our speech:

1. Keep it short!
2. Keep it godly!

Only say what God wants you to say instead of voicing your opinion. Our words matter!!!

"Death and life are in the power of the tongue: and they that love it shall eat the fruit thereof." Proverbs 18:21

Speaking words of life means speaking the words of God from scripture. Only speak the things God wants you to speak in 2024.

Say Only What God Wants
You to Say In 2024

DEUTERONOMY 24
AVOID DIVORCE

Here in Deuteronomy 24, Moses discusses the issue of marriage, divorce, and remarriage among the people in Israel. These scriptures address the case of a woman who has been married, divorced, married to another man, and either divorced again or became widowed. The main point of this law was that the first husband, once he had divorced his wife, could not take her back after she had been married to a second husband. Jewish tradition considered it a form of "wife swapping" and exploitation of the wife. In Matthew 19:7-9, the disciples asked Jesus about these scriptures in Deuteronomy 24. Jesus' response was to only divorce in the case of sexual immorality. Now, just because you can divorce does not mean you have to.

The option is left up to the individual who has been sinned against.

Make no mistake about it, "God hates divorce." So, let us do what is necessary to avoid infidelity and do what is needed to improve our marriages before they end up in divorce. I have been happily married for 25 years straight to the same beautiful woman. We often get asked, "What are some keys to a successful marriage?" Here are a few keys that I want to share with you to help your relationship to prosper.

Ten Keys to Good Marriages

1. Seek to always out-serve your spouse.
2. Liking your spouse is as important as loving your spouse.
3. Forgiveness!
4. Be willing to adapt.
5. Do not seek to be right; seek to do right.
6. Never be alone with the opposite sex.
7. Seek to understand instead of being understood.
8. Look for the positives in your spouse and not the negatives.
9. Make God the center of your marriage that everything else revolves around.
10. Love your wife and respect your husband.

This is not an all-inclusive list, but it is a great start. Curse divorce and do whatever is necessary to avoid it. Do not even threaten or use the "D" word in your marriage. The devil loves divorce and division, so do what is needed to improve your marriage in 2024.

Avoid Divorce In 2024

JOSHUA 24
BE SOLD OUT TO JESUS

This chapter contains the last recorded words of this great warrior we know as Joshua. He gathers all the tribes of Israel in Shechem to remind them of the victories God has given them in the past. He shows them the importance of staying fully connected to God in the future.

Joshua's Final Instructions

1. Fear God, v.14
2. Worship God, v.14
3. Stay committed to God, v.14
4. Get rid of things that do not glorify God, v.14

5. Be single-minded in your dedication to God, v.15
6. Do not play games with God, v.19
7. Keep your covenant with God, v.22-27

After this last sermon, Joshua passed away after living to be 110 years old. Joshua was a warrior, a worshiper, and was wholeheartedly committed to the Lord.

Be Sold Out to Jesus in 2024

1 SAMUEL 24
DEMONSTRATE TEMPERANCE

After several failed attempts by Saul to kill David, David finally has the opportunity to retaliate against Saul and kill him. However, David forgoes the chance to take Saul out and chooses restraint over revenge. To restrain yourself is to have control over the expression of one's emotions. It is disciplining your flesh and allowing the Spirit to control your actions. You cannot do the right thing in your flesh; you need the Holy Spirit to help you.

"Then he answered and spake unto me, saying, This is the word of the Lord unto Zerubbabel, saying, Not by might, nor by power, but by my spirit, saith the Lord of hosts." Zechariah 4:6

Self-control is a fruit of the Spirit called temperance. We certainly need more self-control and temperance in our world today. Temperance is connected to the word "temperature". What is your emotional temperature? Angry, sad, happy? God wants us to be balanced and moderate in our behavior. People who are temperate hold themselves accountable for their actions and restrain themselves from behaving inappropriately when their buttons are pushed or their flesh is tempted.

Five Biblical Facts About Temperance

1. Temperance is a prerequisite to patience.

    "And beside this, giving all diligence, add to your faith virtue; and to virtue knowledge; And to knowledge temperance; and to temperance patience; and to patience godliness;" 2 Peter 1:5-6

    It is hard to be patient with others when you cannot be patient with yourself.

2. Temperance helps us to recognize and reject ungodliness.

'Teaching us that, denying ungodliness and worldly lusts, we should live soberly, righteously, and godly, in this present world;" Titus 2:12

Having self-control gives us discernment in knowing what to say "yes" or "no" to in our lives.

3. Temperance helps us to control our food-binging and gluttony.

"Hast thou found honey? eat so much as is sufficient for thee, lest thou be filled therewith, and vomit it." Proverbs 25:16

Overeating and self-medicating through eating is not just a disorder, it can turn into sin.

4. Temperance helps us to overcome the devil.

"Be sober, be vigilant; because your adversary the devil, as a roaring lion, walketh about, seeking whom he may devour:" 1 Peter 5:8

The devil wants us to indulge or go overboard in fulfilling our earthly desires.

5. Temperance is required in order to be a good leader.

    "A bishop then must be blameless, the husband of one wife, vigilant, sober, of good behaviour, given to hospitality, apt to teach;" 1 Timothy 3:2

    Leaders must have self-control in order to be successful.

Just as David demonstrated restraint and self-control, we need to do the same. Praying for temperance should be at the top of your personal prayer list in 2024.

Demonstrate Temperance In 2024

2 SAMUEL 24
MAKE GODLY DECISIONS

David is determined to take a census and count the number of people in Israel. He was doing it for selfish reasons to have others be impressed with his success. He did this in disobedience to God and although he repented, there were still consequences for his disobedience. God actually let David decide his own punishment. God gave David three options:

- Seven years of famine
- Flee three months before his enemies
- Three days of plague in the land

David chose the three days of plague in the land, but he was extremely upset because he knew his bad decision did not just affect him but an entire nation. Seventy thousand people died because of David's selfish decision.

God wants us to make good decisions and godly decisions in 2024. In order to make better decisions we must do three important things:

1. Pray
   "And whatsoever ye shall ask in my name, that will I do, that the Father may be glorified in the Son." John 14:13

2. Use the Bible

"All scripture is given by inspiration of God, and is profitable for doctrine, for reproof, for correction, for instruction in righteousness:"
2 Timothy 3:16

3. Seek godly counsel

"Where no counsel is, the people fall: but in the multitude of counsellors there is safety."
Proverbs 11:14

Let this year be a year where you go to God and seek His perfect will. Do not just make a decision and hope for the best. Do not deceive yourself into believing that God will bless your bad decisions. Pray, use the Bible, and seek godly advice before making a decision to avoid judgment and experience the blessing of God.

Make Godly Decisions In 2024

2 KINGS 24
LEAD GODLY

This chapter is a reminder that obedience to God's commands is important, and persistent disobedience leads to eventual downfall. It also emphasizes the importance of leaders in developing the moral and spiritual health of a nation. As goes the leaders, so goes the followers. Here in 2 Kings 24, King Jehoiakim of Judah is rebelling against Nebuchadnezzar, king of Babylon, after three years of service. King Jehoiakim's son, Jehoiachin, ascends the throne and continues his father's evil ways in the nation. This chapter really is the beginning of the end of the kingdom of Judah because of their continual disobedience to God. Sin has consequences.

"For the wages of sin is death; but the gift of God is eternal life through Jesus Christ our Lord." Romans 6:23

The consequence of Judah's sin was total destruction and annihilation. As leaders, it is important to lead people to the Lord and into righteousness.

Ten Jobs of a Leader

1. Leaders serve.
2. Leaders love.
3. Leaders inspire.
4. Leaders direct.

5. Leaders live holy lives.
6. Leaders are learners.
7. Leaders are prayer warriors.
8. Leaders lead.
9. Leaders motivate.
10. Leaders have integrity.

I could give you ten more jobs of leader, but we will stop there. Leaders will face greater judgment than followers when they stand before the Lord, so do not be quick to want to be in charge. Leadership should humble you, not make you feel like the "big man on campus".

Lead Godly In 2024

1 CHRONICLES 24
BE OF GODLY SERVICE

In one word, this chapter is about "service". God wants us to be involved in our churches and seek to serve. Instruction plus involvement equals growth.

Six Reasons Why Serving and Being Involved in Church is Important

1. Serving others helps us to grow in Christ.
2. Serving others helps us to discover our destiny.
3. Serving others helps us to activate our gifts.
4. Serving others helps us to follow Jesus' example of service.
5. Serving others helps us to use our time wisely.
6. Serving others helps us to build the kingdom of God.

Serving others is a command, but it also brings joy when you can make a difference in someone's life. Seek to serve others like never before in 2024.

Be of Godly Service In 2024

2 CHRONICLES 24
BE A FINISHER

Joash was seven years old when he became king and he reigned for 40 years. The Bible said he did what was right in the sight of the Lord all the days of Jehoiada the priest. This implies that when Jehoiada died, Joash no longer did what was right in the sight of the Lord. This chapter documents that Joash turned to idolatry when Jehoiada died. What is sad is that he started out strong but finished weak. God wants us to be finishers and end the race strong, not with weakness.

Five Facts About Finishers

1. Jesus is a finisher.

   His final words on the cross were, "it is finished". When God begins a work inside of us, His desire is to complete what He started. Jesus is the author and finisher of our faith.

2. Non-finishers are disqualified for kingdom use.

   The Bible says we must endure till the end and cross the finish line in order to be saved.

3. Finishers are fighters.

   Finishers fight the devil like a boxer in a ring or a UFC fighter in the octagon.

4. Quitters never win, and winners never quit.
    Quitting is never an option for the true child
    of God.

5. Finishers are faithful.
    Faithfulness is probably the most important
    quality we can have that proves our love for
    Christ.

    Joash did not finish strong. He finished weak.
God desires for us to start strong and finish stronger.
Paul said in 2 Timothy 4:7, *"I have fought a good
fight, I have finished my course, I have kept the
faith:"* Paul ran to win and to cross the finish line.
He kept the faith regardless of what the enemy did
or what God allowed. Do not start and stop. Do not
even start and slow down. Start strong and finish
strong.

Be A Finisher In 2024

JOB 24
BE MORE POSITIVE

    Job has definitely gone through and
experienced a lot of loss in his life up to this point.

He is dealing with a little depression, and he is looking at the world through cynical eyes. He is being pessimistic and negative. In some ways, Job is starting to allow the negativity of his so-called "friends" to begin to affect him. He is talking about subjects like …

- how the wicked abuse the powerless
- how the wicked go unpunished
- how the wicked are selfish
- how the wicked are prospering

And in verse 12, Job asks, "Where is God while all this is going on?" Be careful who you hang around because you will become a product of your environment.

"Be not deceived: evil communications corrupt good manners." 1 Corinthians 15:33

You may go through some things that are hard and tough in 2024, but do not let cynicism creep into your heart. Do not start wondering if God is there and if God really cares. Yes, God is there and yes, God cares. Work at being more positive even in a negative world. Do not allow pessimism to rule your mind. God is not going to leave you nor forsake you. God will make the impossible…

possible. Keeping your focus on God and your eyes on the Word of God helps you to stay positive. It takes no faith to be negative in negative times. It does take faith to trust God when things are not going so well. Keep your eyes on Jesus and know God will make a way.

Be Positive In 2024

PSALM 24
GET INTO THE PRESENCE OF THE LORD

Psalm 24 is a smaller psalm with only ten verses, but its message is very clear. The Lord is the owner of everything on Earth because He is the creator of everything on Earth. He even created us, and if we are to prosper, we must stay connected to Him. The question is asked, "Who shall abide in God's presence?" or "Who will God invite into His presence?" The answer is simple and found in verse 4, *"He that hath clean hands, and a pure heart; who hath not lifted up his soul unto vanity, nor sworn deceitfully."*

Four Kinds of People God Allows
into His Presence

1. Those with clean hands

    Clean hands literally means to have no dirty
    dealings.

2. Those with pure hearts

    A pure heart is not just about what you do but
    the motives that are attached to what you do.

3. Those with humble souls

    Humility refers to not walking in pride and
    not trusting in ourselves.

4. Those with honest intentions

    We cannot judge others by their actions and
    then expect them to judge us by our
    intentions.

Let us follow the instructions of David and do
whatever is necessary to get into and stay in the
presence of the Lord.

Get Into the Presence of the Lord In 2024

PROVERBS 24
NEW YEAR'S COMMITMENTS

As always, this proverb, like most of the other proverbs, is full of individual sermon sentences that in many ways provide us with an opportunity to establish some New Years' commitments. Having direction and establishing a vision is a great way to start a year. Proverbs 24 definitely gives us words of wisdom to ensure a successful year.

15 New Year's Commitments for 2024

1. Do not envy evil people, v.1-2
2. Seek wisdom, v.3-6
3. Avoid sinning, v.7-9
4. Pray for strength in adversity, v.10
5. Reach out and help others, v.11-12
6. Eat healthy, v.13-14
7. Be resilient, v.15-16
8. Do not rejoice when your enemies fail or fall, v.17-18
9. Do not worry, v.19-20
10. Respect God, v.21-22
11. Be impartial, v.23-25
12. Respond correctly, v.26
13. Be prepared, v.27
14. Speak the truth, v.28-29

15. Do not be lazy, v.30-34

Proverbs 24 gives us 15 things to do to start out the year correctly. These are 15 commitments we all can make to better ourselves in the new year.

Make A New Years Commitment to Begin In 2024

ISAIAH 24
BE A PROMISE-KEEPER

God is bringing judgement upon the people because they have not kept their word and have broken their covenant with God.

Four Facts About Not Keeping Your Vows

1. Breaking a vow is lying.
2. Breaking a vow is worse than not making a vow.
3. Breaking a vow is a sin.
4. Breaking a vow brings a self-inflicted curse upon your life.

As Christians, we should be promise-keepers, not promise-breakers. Do not make vows you cannot keep!!!

Be A Promise-Keeper In 2024

JEREMIAH 24
EVERYTHING IS FATHER-FILTERED

The prophet saw two baskets of figs set before him in the temple. The figs in one basket were very good, and the figs in the other basket were very bad. The figs represented the two things that could happen to Israel as they were in captivity. They could accept it as part of God's overall plan and allow their time in captivity to make them better, or they could be mad at God for allowing the captivity, and it would cause their fruit to rot.

One of the toughest lessons to learn as a Christian is that everything is Father-filtered. In other words, when you are connected to Christ, everything that happens must go through the Lord before it manifests in your life. God would not allow anything to happen to His children that, in the long run, would not turn out good as they continue to trust the Lord in the middle of difficult situations.

"And we know that all things work together for good to them that love God, to them who are the called according to his purpose." Romans 8:28

Do not let things you go through in life that you do not understand, or you do not like, make you bitter. Let it make you better. Sometimes our spiritual fruit gets developed more when we have to go through things we do not understand. It is going to rain on the just and the unjust. That is life!!! Be committed to God even through tough times knowing everything is Father-filtered and designed as a part of God's overall plan for our lives.

Everything Is Father-Filtered In 2024

EZEKIEL 24
LOVE GOD NO MATTER WHAT HAPPENS

This is a super hard chapter to swallow as a child of God. God actually uses Ezekiel as a sign to the people and of how he lost his wife and how the people will lose what they love. God told Ezekiel his wife was going to die, and he would use it as a way to teach a lesson to those who refused to turn back to God. God was obviously mad at the evil and rebellion in the world and felt like He needed to go to the extreme to make a point. God felt comfortable enough with Ezekiel's commitment to Him that He felt He could take his wife, and Ezekiel would deal with it and still live for the Lord. That is a lot of confidence that God had in Ezekiel. The Bible says that God is slow to get angry, but when He does get mad, it gets crazy.

What Does God Hate?

1. Pride
2. Liars
3. Murderers
4. Cheaters
5. Immorality
6. Instigators
7. Troublemakers

"These six things doth the Lord hate: yea, seven are an abomination unto him:[17] *A proud look, a lying tongue, and hands that shed innocent blood,*[18] *An heart that deviseth wicked imaginations, feet that be swift in running to mischief,*[19] *A false witness that speaketh lies, and he that soweth discord among brethren."* Proverbs 6:16-19

When God hates something, He goes to extremes to get our attention. In many ways, this is a more disturbing story than God totally destroying the earth. The moral of this chapter is to look at things God does through the lens of eternity. God knew one day Ezekiel would be reunited with his wife. In God's mind, it was a temporary loss for Ezekiel. The loss of the people's souls would be permanent. God looked at her as collateral damage to use to help others to understand the seriousness of obeying God. The hope was Ezekiel's great loss would wake people up and help them to realize that if the great prophet Ezekiel could have something precious taken away by God, they could have something taken away from them as well. Our prayer should be, "God give us the ability to love and serve You know matter what we lose or have to go through in this life."

Love God No Matter What
Happens In 2024

MATTHEW 24
LIVING IN LAST OF LAST DAYS

After Jesus is done lambasting the Pharisees and religious leaders in the previous chapter with their future fate for their hypocrisy, Jesus goes on a field trip with the disciples to begin Matthew 24. As they are walking through Jerusalem, the disciples are impressed with the beautiful buildings that were surrounding them. Jesus was cautioning His disciples to not be impressed by what man builds on the outside but by what God builds on the inside of man. Jesus prophesied that these buildings would be destroyed in part because God was not the one to build it to begin with.

"Except the Lord build the house, they labour in vain that build it: except the Lord keep the city, the watchman waketh but in vain." Psalm 127:1

Then Jesus proceeds to tell them the end of time is near, and He gives them signs to watch as the second coming of the Lord draws near.

11 Signs of the End-Times

1. Unprecedented deception, v.4
2. Wars and rumors of wars, v.6
3. Division among nations, v.7
4. Worldwide famines, v.7
5. Infectious diseases, v.7
6. Earthquakes in strange places, v.7
7. Persecution of the righteous, v.9
8. Hate and betrayal in relationships will occur, v.10
9. False prophets will arise, v.11
10. The love for God will decline, v.12
11. Universal evangelism, v.14

It is easy to see with this short list of signs that the end is near, and Jesus is coming back very soon. The time is now to serve the Lord and prepare for Jesus' soon return.

***We Are Living In The Last
of The Last Days In 2024***

LUKE 24
RESURRECTION POWER

This is the last chapter in the book of Luke, and it ends with the resurrection of our Lord and Savior, Jesus Christ. This story is read in churches all over the world every Easter Sunday morning, but it has daily relevance for every Christian.

Why is the Resurrection of Christ Important?

1. Jesus' resurrection means that His sacrificial death on the cross was sufficient for salvation and that our sins can be forgiven.

   "For I delivered unto you first of all that which I also received, how that Christ died for our sins according to the scriptures; And that he was buried, and that he rose again the third day according to the scriptures:" 1 Corinthians 15:3-4

2. Jesus' resurrection demonstrates His victory over Satan, sin, death, hell, and the grave.

   "Whom God hath raised up, having loosed the pains of death: because it was not

possible that he should be holden of it."
Acts 2:24

3. Jesus' resurrection provides us assurance that He now lives to intercede for His people.

   "Wherefore he is able also to save them to the uttermost that come unto God by him, seeing he ever liveth to make intercession for them."
   Hebrews 7:25

4. Jesus' resurrection releases the same power in our lives that raised Christ from the dead.

   "But if the Spirit of him that raised up Jesus from the dead dwell in you, he that raised up Christ from the dead shall also quicken your mortal bodies by his Spirit that dwelleth in you." Romans 8:11

Without the resurrection of Christ, we would have no hope!!! Do not allow yourself to focus on the power of the resurrection on only one day this year. The resurrection of Christ is relevant every day. So, activate the resurrection power of Christ in your life every day!

Resurrection Power In 2024

ACTS 24
BE A SPIRITUAL PEST

Oh do 1 love this chapter! In verse five, it describes Paul as a "pestilent fellow". The religious and political leaders considered Paul a spiritual pest. A pest is something that annoys, frustrates, aggravates, and is a nuisance to others. I would like to say they falsely accused him. Although there were false claims on this charge, he was definitely guilty. Tertullus, a lawyer hired by the Sanhedrin, is trying to convince Governor Felix that Paul is a threat to the Roman Empire. Tertullus claimed Paul incited riots and caused trouble that was worthy of putting him in jail or even him being sentenced to death. Religious people do not want the "pot stirred"; they want the "status quo". They want to stay in their comfort zone. In 2024, we need to stand up for righteousness even if it means we are called "troublemakers" by the world.

What Made Paul a Spiritual Pest?

1. He wanted the approval of God more than he wanted the applause of man.
2. He spoke the truth and refused to back down from those who wanted him to be politically correct.

3. He never allowed suffering to weaken his
    all-out commitment to Christ.
4. He was against anything God was against
    and supported anything God supported.

Quit letting the devil aggravate you, and you
start to aggravate the devil. Be the devil's worst
nightmare by living a sold-out life for Christ in
2024.

***Be A Pest to The Devil In
2024***

Chapter 24's Summary

Genesis 24	= Finding A Spouse
Exodus 24	= Fire of God
Leviticus 24	= Love What God Loves
Numbers 24	= Say Only What God Wants You to Say
Deuteronomy 24	= Avoid Divorce
Joshua 24	= Be Sold-Out to Jesus
1 Samuel 24	= Demonstrate Temperance
2 Samuel 24	= Make Godly Decisions
2 Kings 24	= Lead Godly
1 Chronicles 24	= Be of Godly Service
2 Chronicles 24	= Be A Finisher
Job 24	= Be More Positive
Psalm 24	= Get into the Presence of God
Proverbs 24	= New Year's Commitments
Isaiah 24	= Be A Promise-Keeper
Jeremiah 24	= Everything is Father-Filtered
Ezekiel 24	= Love God No Matter What
Matthew 24	= Last of the Last Days
Luke 24	= Resurrection Power
Acts 24	= Be A Pest to the Devil

Chapter 5
Prophetic Scriptures for 2024

Of the 31,102 verses in the Bible, 19 Scriptures have the number 24 in them. Combined with nine of the 20:24 scriptures and seven of the 24:24 scriptures, we find prophetic insight for 2024. These scriptures help us in developing a vision and provide us with a roadmap as to what is to come this year.

Scriptures that Mention Twenty-Four

Dedication

"And all the oxen for the sacrifice of the peace offerings were twenty and four bullocks, the rams sixty, the he goats sixty, the lambs of the first year sixty. This was the dedication of the altar, after that it was anointed." Numbers 7:88

Dedication is about devotion. God wants us to be single-minded and totally devoted to obeying Him in 2024.

Rarity

"And there was yet a battle in Gath, where was a man of great stature, that had on every hand six fingers, and on every foot six toes, four and twenty in number; and he also was born to the giant."
2 Samuel 21:20

"And yet again there was war at Gath, where was a man of great stature, whose fingers and toes were four and twenty, six on each hand, and six on each foot and he also was the son of the giant."
1 Chronicles 20:6

Things will happen in 2024 that have never happened before. "Once in a lifetime" or "never before" will be phrases that will be popular in 2024.

Rebellion

"In the third year of Asa king of Judah began Baasha the son of Ahijah to reign over all Israel in Tirzah, twenty and four years." 1 Kings 15:33

Rebellion is as witchcraft and must be avoided in order to have success in 2024.

Fasting

"Now in the twenty and fourth day of this month the children of Israel were assembled with fasting, and with sackclothes, and earth upon them."
Nehemiah 9:1

Fasting is a word that is not mentioned much in the church because fasting requires sacrifice. Fasting is still relevant for the Christian today, and is one of the best ways to get our flesh to be in subjection to our Spirit.

Worship

"And round about the throne were four and twenty seats: and upon the seats I saw four and twenty elders sitting, clothed in white raiment; and they had on their heads crowns of gold." Revelation 4:4

"The four and twenty elders fall down before him that sat on the throne, and worship him that liveth for ever and ever, and cast their crowns before the throne, saying," Revelation 4:10

"And when he had taken the book, the four beasts and four and twenty elders fell down before the Lamb, having every one of them harps, and golden vials full of odours, which are the prayers of saints." Revelation 5:8

"And the four beasts said, Amen. And the four and twenty elders fell down and worshipped him that liveth for ever and ever." Revelation 5:14

"And the four and twenty elders, which sat before God on their seats, fell upon their faces, and worshipped God," Revelation 11:16

"And the four and twenty elders and the four beasts fell down and worshipped God that sat on the throne, saying, Amen; Alleluia." Revelation 19:4

Six times the 24 elders are mentioned in the book of Revelation, and every time it is connected to worship. The words "worship" or "worshipped" are used 24 times in the book of Revelation.

Spiritual Order

"The three and twentieth to Delaiah, the four and twentieth to Maaziah."
1 Chronicles 24:18

This scripture refers to the appointed order of who would minister in the temple. Maaziah was the 24th person assigned to serve in the temple. Maaziah was the last one of the Levites to serve. His name means strength. Maybe they were saving the best for last. Good things come when we allow God to order our steps.

Help

"The four and twentieth to Romamtiezer, he, his sons, and his brethren, were twelve." 1 Chronicles 25:31

There were 24 different musicians and Romamtiezer was the 24th and last person mentioned. His name means help. Let this be a year we seek to help and not be the hero.

Divine Appointment

"And in the four and twentieth day of the first month, as I was by the side of the great river, which is Hiddekel;" Daniel 10:4

"In the four and twentieth day of the sixth month, in the second year of Darius the king." Haggai 1:15

"In the four and twentieth day of the ninth month, in the second year of Darius, came the word of the Lord by Haggai the prophet, saying," Haggai 2:10

"And again the word of the Lord came unto Haggai in the four and twentieth day of the month, saying," Haggai 2:20

"Upon the four and twentieth day of the eleventh month, which is the month Sebat, in the second year of Darius, came the word of the Lord unto Zechariah, the son of Berechiah, the son of Iddo the prophet, saying," Zechariah 1:7

This is a year God wants to visit with us every day, but on the 24th of every month, He wants us to have a divine appointment. He has scheduled it into His calendar; make sure you schedule it into your calendar.

Pay Attention

"Consider now from this day and upward, from the four and twentieth day of the ninth month, even from the day that the foundation of the Lord's temple was laid, consider it." Haggai 2:18

Twice in one scripture we are told to "consider" by the prophet. Considering something means to pay careful attention to something. Think before you act in 2024.

20:24 Scriptures

Blessing

"An altar of earth thou shalt make unto me, and shalt sacrifice thereon thy burnt offerings, and thy peace offerings, thy sheep, and thine oxen: in all places where I record my name I will come unto thee, and I will bless thee." Exodus 20:24

God wants to bless us when we walk in obedience to His Word. Position yourself in a place to receive everything the Lord has for you in 2024.

Inheritance

"But I have said unto you, Ye shall inherit their land, and I will give it unto you to possess it, a land that floweth with milk and honey: I am the Lord your God, which have separated you from other people." Leviticus 20:24

This is a year to drive out the previous tenants and stake your claim to the inheritance the Lord has for you. Quit settling for manna and water and start eating the milk and honey from the Promise Land.

Judgement

"And when Judah came toward the watch tower in the wilderness, they looked unto the multitude, and, behold, they were dead bodies fallen to the earth, and none escaped." 2 Chronicles 20:24

Let judgement begin in the house of God, within the hearts of every Christian. God is a God of grace, but He is also a God of judgement.

God is in Control

"Man's goings are of the Lord; how can a man then understand his own way?" Proverbs 20:24

Our steps are ordered of the Lord when we seek to be in right standing with God. Let God be in control in 2024.

Disobedience

"Because they had not executed my judgments, but had despised my statutes, and had polluted my sabbaths, and their eyes were after their fathers' idols." Ezekiel 20:24

Avoid being disobedient in all of your behavior in 2024. Allow your life to be pliable in the hands of God, so obedience will become a little easier.

Division

"And when the ten heard it, they were moved with indignation against the two brethren."
Matthew 20:24

Unfortunately, the division within our country will continue to grow even deeper in 2024. Do your best to walk in unity and be a peacemaker.

Pay Your Taxes

"Shew me a penny. Whose image and superscription hath it? They answered and said, Caesar's." Luke 20:24

Pay your worldly taxes and your spiritual tithes in 2024.

Doubt

"But Thomas, one of the twelve, called Didymus, was not with them when Jesus came." John 20:24

Doubt is having faith in the devil. So, doubt your doubts in 2024.

Determination

"But none of these things move me, neither count I my life dear unto myself, so that I might finish my course with joy, and the ministry, which I have received of the Lord Jesus, to testify the gospel of the grace of God." Acts 20:24

Salvation and deliverance come to those who endure unto the end. Refuse to quit.

24:24 Scriptures

Know God's Voice

"And the people said unto Joshua, The Lord our God will we serve, and his voice will we obey." Joshua 24:24

Knowing God's voice comes from spending time with God and knowing His heart.

Judgement

"For the army of the Syrians came with a small company of men, and the Lord delivered a very great host into their hand, because they had forsaken the Lord God of their fathers. So they executed judgment against Joash." 2 Chronicles 24:24

There are always consequences that come with disobedience.

Humility

"They are exalted for a little while, but are gone and brought low; they are taken out of the way as all other, and cut off as the tops of the ears of corn." Job 24:24

Be a person who walks in humility in 2024. Resist the devil and resist pride throughout this year.

Follow the Godly Signs

"Thus Ezekiel is unto you a sign: according to all that he hath done shall ye do: and when this cometh, ye shall know that I am the Lord God." Ezekiel 24:24

Signs provide direction so pray to God for Him to give you discernment in knowing the right signs to follow.

Deception

"For there shall arise false Christs, and false prophets, and shall shew great signs and wonders; insomuch that, if it were possible, they shall deceive the very elect." Matthew 24:24

Deceit and deception will be at an all-time high in 2024. Always use the Word of God to discern the difference between truth and deception.

Resurrection

"And certain of them which were with us went to the sepulchre and found it even so as the women had said: but him they saw not." Luke 24:24

God is in the resurrection business in 2024. Never forget the same spirit that raised Christ from the dead dwells inside of us.

Faith

"And after certain days, when Felix came with his wife Drusilla, which was a Jewess, he sent for Paul, and heard him concerning the faith in Christ."
Acts 24:24

We need faith in God, not faith in faith in 2024. If you want to please God, you must have faith.

These scriptures are not just thrown in to take up space and add more pages to a book. They are important and relevant to our success in 2024. There is a reason these scriptures are included in this book. They help us to know what to look out for this year. The Word of God is quick and powerful. When we activate and apply the scripture to our lives, it makes us more like Jesus and less like us. Let us work the Word, so the Word will work for us.

Chapter 6
Spiritual Forecast

A New Sound in The Church

People always tell me that one of the highlights of the Prophetic Almanac is the prophetic word that God gives to me every year for our nation. When God gave me this word, I had no idea what the vision of the year would be, but obviously God did and was preparing me earlier than normal for what He wants in 2024. This is a year of worship!!!! So, a few months ago in the middle of the night as I was in pain struggling to pass a kidney stone, the Lord gave me this prophetic word for our nation.

"A new sound is coming from the church that is not some man-made, soulish noise that stirs the flesh but a heaven-sent sound that will shake the earth in preparation for the coming of the Lord. This sound is rising from a place of pain in the hearts of people who have been tested and tried and have not quit or given up. They have held onto God through situations where others have let go. They have not wasted their pain, but have allowed the things that are sometimes unexplainable and uncomfortable to produce a power of God that is releasing a new level of anointing. This sound is

deep calling unto deep. This is the new sound of worship. It is real and it is raw. It is an axe-sharpening sound that will allow you to cut through the darkness of the enemy and break open the hard hearts of mankind to discharge a hope from Heaven that only God can give to the hopeless and the lost. This sound is life. This sound is love. This sound is life changing. This is the new sound of worship. This is a sound that has been heard before in the upper room on the day of Pentecost as 120 people from 17 nations joined together in unity for ten days of continuous prayer and praise until the power of the Holy Spirit was poured out. There have been small pockets of this sound heard from time to time after that day, but those who are spiritually hungry for more of God, are releasing this new sound that has been bombarding the dam between Heaven and Earth; and is forcing My hand to pierce through the barrier, and causing the water of God to burst forth upon the world to heal the sick, save the lost, deliver those who are bound, strengthen the weak, encourage the discouraged, and release an anointing that will destroy every yoke and remove every burden. This new sound will be a funnel from Heaven to Earth to produce a flood from Heaven into your lives that will cause you to become so addicted to My presence that it will sometimes feel like you cannot get enough. It will cause you to love the unlovable, forgive the unforgivable, and not care about the things you do not understand. With every new move of God, there is a new sound of God. When Moses confronted Pharaoh, there emerged a sound of freedom as Moses declared, "let my people go". There was a sound of a little shepherd boy by the name of David that rang out on the mountain sides of Israel when he would worship the Lord all by himself that gave him the ability to conquer a giant as he spoke out against the enemy that would intimidate and create fear in the hearts of God's people. There was a sound that came forth when John the Baptist said, "prepare the way for the coming Messiah" that cried out for people to return to the Lord. And there was a sound that came from the people when Jesus entered Jerusalem days before His death that energized the faithful but ruffled the feathers of the religious that caused Jesus to say, "if My people do not praise Me, the rocks will cry out." And, now according to Acts 15:16 which says, "after this I will return and will build again the tabernacle of David, which is fallen down; and I will build again the ruins thereof, and I will set it up:" I am hearing a sound that is releasing My glory like in the days of old. However, this new sound is not just recognized in Heaven; it is recognized in hell. As much as the Lord loves this sound, the devil hates this sound. This is the new sound of worship. This sound from God's people is a threat to his evil agenda, so prepare for war!!! You will be attacked. All who live godly and all who produce a sound that moves God to release His glory on Earth will be under attack. But remember, greater is He that is in you than he that is in the world. This sound is a seed that has been planted in your spirit and needs to be watered by the Holy Spirit, so you can give birth to a new move of God that will release revival upon the earth. Let worship reign in your private time with Me and let it reign in your corporate times with your fellow believers. This new sound of worship will change you and release My shekinah glory on the earth. "Worship Me," says the Lord!!!"

<u>Southwest Region</u>

States in the Southwest Region and Their Specific "Word" for 2024:

Arizona – Faith
Arkansas – Grace
Colorado – Forgiveness
Louisiana – Intervention
New Mexico – Peace
Oklahoma – Unity
Texas – Devotion

Prayer for the Southwest Region:
Help Me Live It by Keith Green

Oh Lord, You're beautiful. Your face is all I see. For when Your eyes are on this child, Your grace abounds to me. Oh Lord, please light the fire. That once burned bright and clean. Replace the lamp of my first love. That burns with holy fear. I want to take Your Word and shine it all around. But first, help me just to live it, Lord. And when I'm doing well, help me to never seek a crown. For my reward is giving glory to You.

Book of the Bible for the Southwest Region:
Revelation

Scripture for the Southwest Region:
"There hath no temptation taken you but such as is common to man: but God is faithful, who will not suffer you to be tempted above that ye are able; but will with the temptation also make a way to escape, that ye may be able to bear it." 1 Corinthians 10:13

State in the Southwest Region to Watch:
Arkansas

Major City in the Southwest Region to Watch:
Phoenix, Arizona

Key Months for the Southwest Region:
January, May, June, and December

States in the West Region and Their Specific "Word" for 2024:

Alaska – Meditate
California – Worship
Hawaii – Taste
Idaho – Intercession
Montana – Bloom
Nevada – Endurance
Oregon – Balance
Utah – Courage
Washington – Love
Wyoming – Compassion

Prayer for the West Region:
Empty Vessel by Martin Luther

Behold, Lord, an empty vessel that needs to be filled. My Lord, fill it. I am weak in faith; strengthen thou me. I am cold in love; warm me and make me fervent that my love may go out to my neighbor. I do not have a strong and firm faith; at times I doubt and am unable to trust thee altogether. O Lord, help me. Strengthen my faith and trust in thee. In thee, I have sealed the treasures of all I have. I am poor; Thou art rich and didst come to be merciful to the poor. I am a sinner; Thou art upright. With me, there is an abundance of sin; in thee is the fullness of righteousness. Therefore, I will remain with thee of who I can receive but to whom I may not give. Amen.

Book of the Bible for the West Region:
Exodus

Scripture for the West Region:
"I am the vine, ye are the branches: He that abideth in me, and I in him, the same bringeth forth much fruit: for without me ye can do nothing." John 15:5

State in the West Region to Watch:
Hawaii

Major City in the West Region to Watch:
Boise, Idaho

Key Months for the West Region:
January, April, October, and December

States in the Midwest Region and Their Specific "Word" for 2024:

Illinois – Awakening
Indiana – Humility
Iowa – Transformation
Kansas – Surrender
Michigan – Study
Minnesota – Freedom
Missouri – Hope
Nebraska – Patience
North Dakota – Practice
Ohio – Examine
South Dakota – Possess
Wisconsin – Learn

Prayer for the Midwest Region:
Instrument of Your Peace by St. Francis of Assisi

Lord, make me an instrument of Your peace: where there is hatred, let me sow love; where there is injury, pardon; where there is doubt, faith; where there is despair, hope; where there is darkness, light; where there is sadness, joy; O divine Master, grant that I may not so much seek to be consoled as to console, to be understood as to understand, to be loved as to love. For it is in giving that we receive, it is in pardoning that we are pardoned, and it is in dying that we awake to eternal life. Amen

Book of the Bible for the Midwest Region:
Book of James

Scripture for the Midwest Region:
"Study to shew thyself approved unto God, a workman that needeth not to be ashamed, rightly dividing the word of truth." 2 Timothy 2:15

State in the Midwest Region to Watch:
Ohio

Major City in the Midwest Region to Watch:
Detroit, Michigan

Key Months for the Midwest Region:
February, June, and August

<u>**Southeast Region**</u>

States in the Southeast Region and Their Specific "Word" for 2024:
Alabama – Calmness
Florida – Patience

Georgia – Laugh
Kentucky – Grace
Mississippi – Trust
North Carolina – Healing
South Carolina – Overcome
Tennessee – Believe
Virginia – Opportunity
West Virginia – Watch

Prayer for the Southeast Region:
Indwelling of the Spirit by St. Augustine

Holy Spirit, powerful Consoler, sacred Bond of the Father and the Son, Hope of the afflicted, descend into my heart and establish in it Your loving dominion. Enkindle in my tepid soul the fire of Your Love so that I may be wholly subject to you. We believe that when You dwell in us, You also prepare a dwelling for the Father and the Son. Deign, therefore, to come to me, Consoler of abandoned souls, and Protector of the needy. Help the afflicted, strengthen the weak, and support the wavering. Come and purify me. Let no evil desire take possession of me. You love the humble and resist the proud. Come to me, glory of the living, and hope of the dying. Lead me by Your grace that I may always be pleasing to you. Amen.

Book of the Bible for the Southeast Region:
2 Samuel

Scripture for the Southeast Region:
"But ye shall receive power, after that the Holy Ghost is come upon you: and ye shall be witnesses unto me both in Jerusalem, and in all Judaea, and in Samaria, and unto the uttermost part of the earth." Acts 1:8

State in the Southeast Region to Watch:
North Carolina

Major City in the Southeast Region to Watch:
Columbia, South Carolina

Key Months for the Southeast Region:
February, April, October, and November

Northeast Region

States in the Northeast Region and Their Specific "Word" for 2024:
Connecticut – Optimism
Delaware – Activate
Maine – Connect

Maryland – Guard
Massachusetts – Develop
New Hampshire – Character
New Jersey – Rise
New York – Observe
Pennsylvania – Confidence
Rhode Island – Train
Vermont – Seek

Prayer for the Northeast Region:
Covenant Prayer by John Wesley

I am no longer my own, but yours. Put me to what you will, place me with whom you will. Put me to doing, put me to suffering. Let me be put to work for you or set aside for you, praised for you, or criticized for you. Let me be full, let me be empty. Let me have all things, let me have nothing. I freely and fully surrender all things to your glory and service. And now, O wonderful and holy God, Creator, Redeemer, and Sustainer, you are mine, and I am yours. So be it. And the covenant which I have made on earth, let it also be made in heaven. Amen.

Book of the Bible for the Northeast Region:
Gospel of Luke

Scripture for the Northeast Region:
"But the fruit of the Spirit is love, joy, peace, longsuffering, gentleness, goodness, faith, Meekness, temperance: against such there is no law." Galatians 5:22-23

State in the Northeast Region to Watch:
New Hampshire

Major City in the Northeast Region to Watch:
Camden, New Jersey

Key Months for the Northeast Region:
March, July, and September

The Five Regions of the United States

Southwest	West	Midwest	Southeast	Northeast
Arizona	Alaska	Illinois	Alabama	Connecticut
Arkansas	California	Indiana	Florida	Delaware
Colorado	Hawaii	Iowa	Georgia	Maine
Louisiana	Idaho	Kansas	Kentucky	Maryland
New Mexico	Montana	Michigan	Mississippi	Massachusettes
Oklahoma	Nevada	Minnesota	North Carolina	New Hampshire
Texas	Oregon	Missouri	South Carolina	New Jersey
	Utah	Nebraska	Tennessee	New York
	Washington	North Dakota	Virginia	Pennsylvania
	Wyoming	Ohio	West Virginia	Rhode Island
		South Dakota		Vermont
		Wisconsin		

Chapter 7
24th Day People

If you have a birthday on the 24th day of any month, then this chapter is specifically for you. God is wanting this to be the best year of your life. In order for that to happen, your cooperation is necessary. You must understand the need you have for God in your life. You can do that by not thinking you have all the answers and can fix all the problems of life. You have to depend on God and not be so independent and stubborn in your beliefs. Let God be in charge and know He will not fail you. Your mind is so complex; it complicates your future when you think too much. What you are thinking and dwelling on dictates your belief system whether it is true or not. The Lord wants you to walk in truth and reality, not deception and fantasy.

You have to call out to the Lord for help. "Help" is actually the best prayer you can pray. Ask God to help you "control", not "kill" your emotions, so your emotions do not lead you to commit actions that are detrimental to your future. Get your new wineskin on for the new things the Lord is wanting to bring to you in your life in 2024: new ideas, new experiences, and new people. Do not allow your fear, anxiety, suspicion, and insecurity to keep you from having the best the Lord has to offer you. As the Lord declared to Joshua, He is speaking to all 24th day people the words of Joshua 1:9, *"Have not I commanded thee? Be strong and of a good courage; be not afraid, neither be thou dismayed: for the Lord thy God is with thee whithersoever thou goest."* Trust God to take you on an adventure of a lifetime. It will bring a smile to your face and joy in your heart.

Traits of 24th Day People

Positive	**Negative**
– Confident	– Manipulative
– Decisive	– Moody
– Faithful	– Pessimistic
– Sensitive	– Overly Involved
– Sentimental	– Emotional
– Talented	– Dramatic
– Organized	– Worrier
– Practical	– Complicated

"Be careful for nothing; but in every thing by prayer and supplication with thanksgiving let your requests be made known unto God." Philippians 4:6

Eight Keys to Success for 24th Day People

1. Let go, and let God be in control.

2. Guard your heart.
3. Stop trying to fix those who do not want help.
4. Control your emotions, or your emotions will control you.
5. Simplify your life.
6. Do not overthink or overcomplicate God's instructions.
7. Be open to new adventures.
8. Get closer to God.

Below is a list of some famous people who have a birthday on the 24th day of the month:

JANUARY 24TH

Mary Lou Retton, Gymnast

Neil Diamond, Singer

Ed Helms, Actor

Ernest Borgnine, Actor

Oral Roberts, Televangelist

Aaron Neville, Singer

John Belushi, Actor

Sean McVay, NFL Coach

FEBRUARY 24th

George Thorogood, Musician

Floyd Mayweather, Boxer

Steve Jobs, Entrepreneur
Honus Wagner, Baseball Hall of Fame
Eddie Murray, MLB Hall of Fame
Edward James Olmos, Actor

MARCH 24TH
Harry Houdini, Magician
Joseph Barbera, Cartoonist
Steve McQueen, Actor
Tommy Hilfiger, Designer
Mark Calaway "The Undertaker", Wrestler
Peyton Manning, NFL Quarterback

APRIL 24th
Kelly Clarkson, Singer
Barbara Streisand, Actress
Cedric the Entertainer, Actor/Comedian
Danny Gokey, Musician
Chipper Jones, NBA Player
Shirley MacLaine, Actress
Richard M. Daley, Politician
Michael O'Keefe, Actor

MAY 24th

Julius Caesar, Roman Emperor
Queen Victoria, United Kingdom Queen
Bob Dylan, Musician
Patti LaBelle, Singer
Priscilla Presley, Actress
Rosanne Cash, Singer
John C. Reilly, Actor
Heavy D, Rapper
Ben "Yahtzee" Croshaw, Videogame Creator

JUNE 24th

Robert Downey Sr., Filmmaker
Jack Dempsey, Boxer
Jeff Beck, Musician
Mick Fleetwood, Musician
Lionel Messi, Argentine Soccer Player

JULY 24th

Amelia Earhart, Aviator
Pam Tillis, Singer
Karl Malone, Basketball Hall of Fame
Jennifer Lopez, Actress/Singer
Elizabeth Moss, Actress
Kristin Chenoweth, Broadway Actress

<u>**AUGUST 24th**</u>

Carlo Gambino, Mafia
Mike Shanahan, Football Coach
Mike Huckabee, Politician
Stephen Fry, Comedian
Steve Guttenberg, Actor
Cal Ripken Jr., Baseball Hall of Fame
Mary Ellen Weber, NASA Astronaut
Marlee Matlin, Deaf Actress
Dave Chappelle, Comedian
Vince McMahon, Entertainer
Reggie Miller, Basketball Player

<u>**SEPTEMBER 24th**</u>

Jim Henson, Puppeteer/Filmmaker
Linda McCartney, Musician
Stephanie McMahon, Wrestler
Eddie George, College Football Hall of Fame

<u>**OCTOBER 24th**</u>

Drake, Rapper
F. Murray Abraham, Actor
Kevin Kline, Actor
Sean O'Malley, MMA Fighter

<u>**NOVEMBER 24th**</u>
Katherine Heigl, Actress
Zachary Taylor, 12th US President
Charles "Lucky" Luciano, Mafia
Oscar Robertson, NBA Guard
Steve Yeager, MLB

<u>**DECEMBER 24th**</u>
Howard Hughes, Reclusive Billionaire
Ava Gardner, Actress
George Patton IV, US General
Anthony Fauci, Immunologist
Kate Spade, Fashion Designer
Ricky Martin, Singer
Ryan Seacrest, TV Host
Davante Adams, NFL Player

Prayer for the 24th Day People

I pray for those who have a birthday on the 24th day of any month in this year. Help them to let go of the things of the past and trust God like never before in 2024. Give them courage to address things within themselves that need to be changed, so they can be more like Jesus. Let their confidence not turn into cockiness that others will perceive as pride. Do not let them overthink the simple instructions of the Lord. Do not let them forget what may be impossible with man, is possible with God. Help them to be open to new relationships that will provide the companionship that they are longing for in their life.

I pray You help them put their flesh in subjection to their spirits and guide them in truth of the Word of God. Protect them from harm and danger. Let no weapon formed against them prosper. Give them wisdom and help them to grow deeper in the knowledge of God. I rebuke all lukewarmness and apathy and pray You would energize their souls to produce more for the Lord in 2024 than ever before. In Jesus' name… AMEN.

Chapter 8
Calendar

JANUARY

- National Blood Donor Month
- National Hobby Month
- National Hot Tea Month
- National Slavery and Human Trafficking Prevention Month
- National Soup Month

Jan 1 - New Year's Day
Jan 6 - Epiphany
Jan 15 - Martin Luther King Jr. Day

FEBRUARY

- American Heart Month
- Black History Month
- National Bake for Family Fun Month
- National Hot Breakfast Month
- National Library Lover's Month
- National Snack Food Month

Feb 1 - National Freedom Day
Feb 2 - Groundhog Day
Feb 2 - National Wear Red Day

Feb 4 - Rosa Parks Day
Feb 10 - Chinese New Year
Feb 11 - Super Bowl
Feb 12 - President Lincoln's Birthday
Feb 13 - Fat Tuesday/Mardi Gras
Feb 14 - Ash Wednesday
Feb 14 - Valentine's Day
Feb 15 - Susan B. Anthony's Birthday
Feb 19 - Presidents' Day

MARCH

- Irish American Heritage Month
- Multiple Sclerosis Awareness Month
- National Caffeine Awareness Month
- National Brain Injury Awareness Month
- National Nutrition Month
- Women's Awareness Month

Mar 1 - Read Across America Day
Mar 1 - Employee Appreciation Day
Mar 10 - Daylight Saving Time starts
Mar 17 - St. Patrick's Day
Mar 19 - Spring Begins
Mar 24 - Purim
Mar 24 - Palm Sunday
Mar 28 - Maundy Thursday
Mar 29 - Good Friday
Mar 29 - Vietnam War Veterans Day

Mar 30 - Holy Saturday
Mar 31 - Easter Sunday

APRIL

- National Month of Hope
- Distracted Driving Awareness Month
- National Child Abuse Awareness Month
- Keep America Beautiful Month
- National Autism Awareness Month
- National Parkinson Awareness Month
- National Pecan Month
- National Volunteer Month

Apr 13 - Thomas Jefferson's Birthday
Apr 15 - Boston Marathon
Apr 15 - Tax Day
Apr 22 - Passover (first day)
Apr 24 - Administrative Professionals Day
Apr 25 - Take your Child to Work Day
Apr 26 - Arbor Day
Apr 30 - Passover (last day)

MAY

- National Dental Care Awareness Month
- National Military Appreciation Month
- National Motorcycle Awareness Month

- Date Your Mate Month
- National Barbecue Month
- National Blood Pressure Month
- National Hamburger Month

May 2 - National Day of Prayer
May 3 - Kentucky Oaks
May 4 - Kentucky Derby
May 4 - Kent State Shootings Remembrance
May 5 - Cinco de Mayo
May 6 - National Nurses Day
May 7 - Teacher Appreciation Day
May 9 - Ascension Day
May 10 - Military Spouse Appreciation Day
May 12 - Mother's Day
May 15 - Peace Officers Memorial Day
May 18 - Armed Forces Day
May 19 - Pentecost
May 22 - Emergency Medical Services for
              Children Day
May 25 - National Missing Children's Day
May 26 - Trinity Sunday
May 27 - Memorial Day

JUNE

- Aquarium Month
- Men's Health Month
- National Fresh Fruit and Vegetables Month

- National Candy Month
- National Great Outdoors Month

Jun 6 - D-Day
Jun 8 - Belmont Stakes
Jun 11 - Shavuot
Jun 14 - Flag Day
Jun 14 - Army Birthday
Jun 16 - Father's Day
Jun 17 - Bunker Hill Day
Jun 19 - Juneteenth
Jun 20 - American Eagle Day
Jun 20 - Summer Begins

JULY

- National Baked Bean Month
- National Cell Phone Courtesy Month
- National Hot Dog Month
- National Ice Cream Month
- National Picnic Month

Jul 4 - Independence Day
Jul 27 - Korean War Veterans Armistice Day
Jul 28 - Parents' Day

AUGUST

- National Wellness Month
- Family Fun Month
- National Eye Exam Month
- National Golf Month
- National Sandwich Month

Aug 4 - Coast Guard Birthday
Aug 7 - Purple Heart Day
Aug 18 - National Senior Citizens Day
Aug 19 - National Aviation Day
Aug 26 - Women's Equality Day

SEPTEMBER

- Baby Safety Month
- Classical Music Month
- National Potato Month
- National Preparedness Month
- National Suicide Prevention Month

Sep 2 - Labor Day
Sep 8 - National Grandparents Day
Sep 11 - Patriot Day
Sep 17 - Constitution Day & Citizenship Day
Sep 18 - Air Force Birthday
Sep 20 - POW/MIA Recognition Day
Sep 22 - Fall Begins

Sep 27 - Native Americans' Day

<u>OCTOBER</u>

- Breast Cancer Awareness Month
- Church Safety and Security Month
- Financial Planning Month
- National Book Month
- National Dessert Month

Oct 2 - Rosh Hashana
Oct 7 - Child Health Day
Oct 12 - Yom Kippur
Oct 13 - Navy Birthday
Oct 14 - Columbus Day
Oct 16 - Boss' Day
Oct 16 - First Day of Sukkot
Oct 19 - Sweetest Day
Oct 23 - Last Day of Sukkot
Oct 24 - Simchat Torah
Oct 31 - Halloween

<u>NOVEMBER</u>

- National Adoption Month
- National Diabetes Month
- National Peanut Butter Lovers Month
- NoSHAVEmber (US – Beard Month)

Nov 1 - All Saints' Day
Nov 2 - All Souls' Day
Nov 3 - Daylight Saving Time Ends
Nov 3 - New York City Marathon
Nov 5 - Election Day
Nov 10 - Marine Corps Birthday
Nov 11 - Veterans Day
Nov 28 - Thanksgiving Day
Nov 29 - Black Friday

DECEMBER

- AIDS Awareness Month
- National Human Rights Month
- Spiritual Literacy Month

Dec 1 - Rosa Parks Day
Dec 1 - First Sunday of Advent
Dec 2 - Cyber Monday
Dec 3 - Giving Tuesday
Dec 7 - Pearl Harbor Remembrance Day
Dec 13 - National Guard Birthday
Dec 21 - Winter Begins
Dec 24 - Christmas Eve
Dec 25 - Christmas Day
Dec 25 - Chanukah/Hanukkah Begins
Dec 31 - New Year's Eve

The calendar information is taken from timeanddate.com

Chapter 9
Journaling for Jesus in 2024

With all our modern technology like phones and computers, personal journaling has taken a back seat to other forms of communication. We text and email others, but really have no personal conversations with ourselves. In many ways, journaling is texting and emailing yourself. It is a form of personal journalism where you give an account of day-to-day events in your life. It is a record of experiences, ideas, lessons, thoughts, or reflections kept regularly for private use to help you remember and recall certain things for future use.

There is no doubt in my mind that God is calling the church to renew its desire to develop a personal journal. Whether it is taking notes in church, or writing things down that you hear from the Lord in prayer, journaling will help you to show God you are serious about serving Him. Do not just go through the motions, but tangibly do something by taking the time to write and document what God is saying to you. As you document your encounters with the Lord, not only will you be strengthened, but He will be able to trust you more with His Word. I have given you 12 prophetic days in 2024 instead of 24. Part of the reason is, I believe the Lord is going to give you a double dose of a prophetic word on the 24th of every month. Be sure to document anything God is saying and doing on these important dates.

1. Wednesday, January 24, 2024

____

____

____

____

2. Saturday, February 24, 2024

____

____

____

____

3. Sunday, March 24, 2024

____

____

____

____

4. Wednesday, April 24, 2024

____

____

____

____

5. Friday, May 24, 2024

____

____

____

____

6. Monday, June 24, 2024

____

____

____

____

7. Wednesday, July 24, 2024

____

____

____

____

8. Saturday, August 24, 2024

____

____

____

____

9. Tuesday, September 24, 2024

____

____

____

____

10. Thursday, October 24, 2024

____

____

____

____

11. Sunday, November 24, 2024

____

____

____

____

12. Tuesday, December 24, 2024

____

____

____

____

Write out any other dates that may mean something to you:

Date   Notes

____

____

____

____

____

____

____

____

____

____

____

____

____

____

____

____

____

____

____

____

____

____

____

Write out any other dates that may mean something
to you:

Date   Notes

____

____

____

____

____

____

____

____

____

____

____

____

____

____

____

____

____

____

____

____

Conclusion

This is going to be a uniquely different year than most, so your obedience to the commands of God is required to enjoy success. This book is your handbook to help guide you and remind you of what is to come. Use the words on these pages to be a spiritual GPS to get you from where you are to where God wants you to be. Things do not always happen overnight. Sometimes things take longer than we want to manifest in our lives.

God always reveals His will progressively, one step at a time, in a very systematic way. He never dots all the "i's" or crosses all the "t's". We would not need faith if we knew everything that is to come. Faith is the only thing that moves and pleases God. So, in lieu of God telling us everything in advance, we have this book to give us a taste or sampling of what is to come. It is going to be an unpredictable year so expect the unexpected. What you see is not always what you will get. "Surprises" and "suddenlys" will dominate in 2024. I heard the Lord say, *to expect "surprises" in the natural and "suddenlys" in the spiritual."* The world will be shocked by the surprises that will arise throughout this year. In science, AI, technology, space, and even in the medical fields, there will be advances that will thrill, excite, and stun the universe. The "suddenlys" are for My faithful followers who have felt I am slow in fulfilling My promises. Delay has not meant denial; I will keep My word and bring every promise to pass. You will experience the suddenness of My glory releasing you from a life of endurance to a life of endless blessing.

Just as there are 24 hours that make up a complete day, it seems to me, in the spiritual realm, that the number 24 is an opportunity to bring closure to the things of the past and write a new chapter in your personal book of life.

"Therefore if any man be in Christ, he is a new creature: old things are passed away; behold, all things are become new." 2 Corinthians 5:17

As I conclude this book, let me give you a few important thoughts for 2024 that I feel the Lord wants me share to help you navigate throughout this year.

Ten Commandments For 2024

1. Take one day at a time.
2. Your superpower is being you.
3. Instead of being a teacher, be a better student.
4. Do not look back, look forward.

5. Do not fear the future.
6. Be nice to everyone.
7. Challenge yourself more.
8. Worship God every day.
9. Forgive yourself and others.
10. Never quit!

The Prophetic Almanac 2024 is designed to help you know what to expect of God, and to inform you of what God expects of you. Apply the truths of this book and take advantage of the open doors that are before you. Obey God and worship God to experience God's best for your life in 2024!

More of God In 2024

To get daily wisdom nuggets, check out Pastor Bill on social media for the most important minute of your day!

The Minute That Matters

Scan the QR code with your phone, and you will be automatically connected to your choice of social media.